THAT'S

Life

DEBBIE JANE

Paperback: 978-1-969919-39-8
Hardcover: 978-1-969919-80-0
eBook: 978-1-969919-40-4
Library of Congress Control Number: 2025922619

This is a work of nonfiction.

Ordering Information:

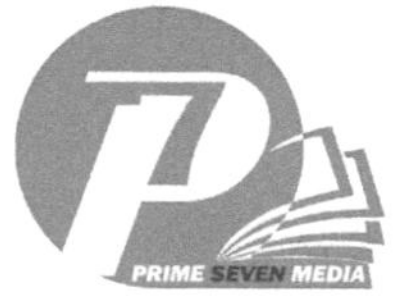

Prime Seven Media
518 Landmann St.
Tomah City, WI 54660

Printed in the United States of America

GIVING THANKS.

I give thanks to everyone who read my first book. (susurrar en el viento).

I give thanks to everyone who has walked by my side during these years of challenges,

As the world has taken a turn we did not expect.

With the knowledge we already know, we can continue advancing in our growth.

In caring for the planet and nurturing it, so that it stops crying. Hug the trees, lie in the sea, jump into the void. Scream so that Mother Nature hears you and knows that she is not alone and that we can change."or not"?

THE MADNESS OF A WRITER.

At night, she would tiptoe down the hallway
like a mouse.
Nibbling on her thoughts,
with the lights dim, as not to wake anyone,
she sits in her chair, turns on the computer and writes,
The ideas come flowing at night when everyone is asleep.
You can only hear in the distance the tip tip like a mouse
nibbling on a piece of cheese.

HAPPINESS

Happiness is having fun,
in rainbow muddy puddles.

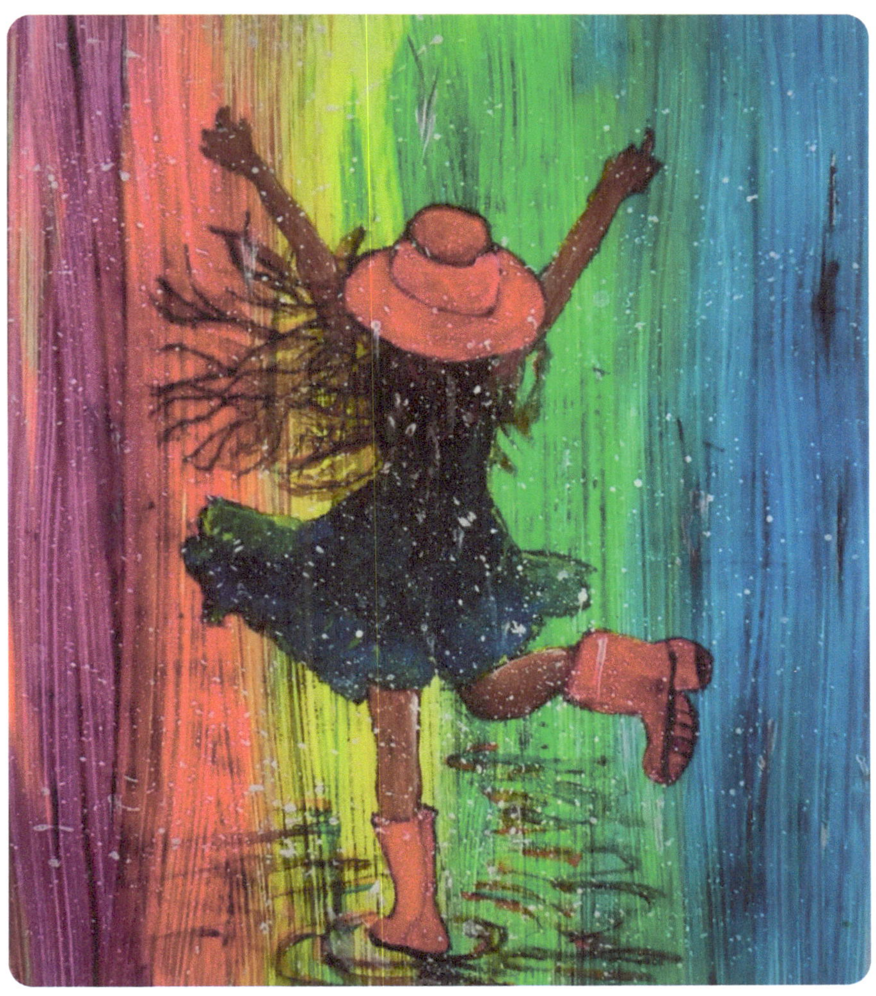

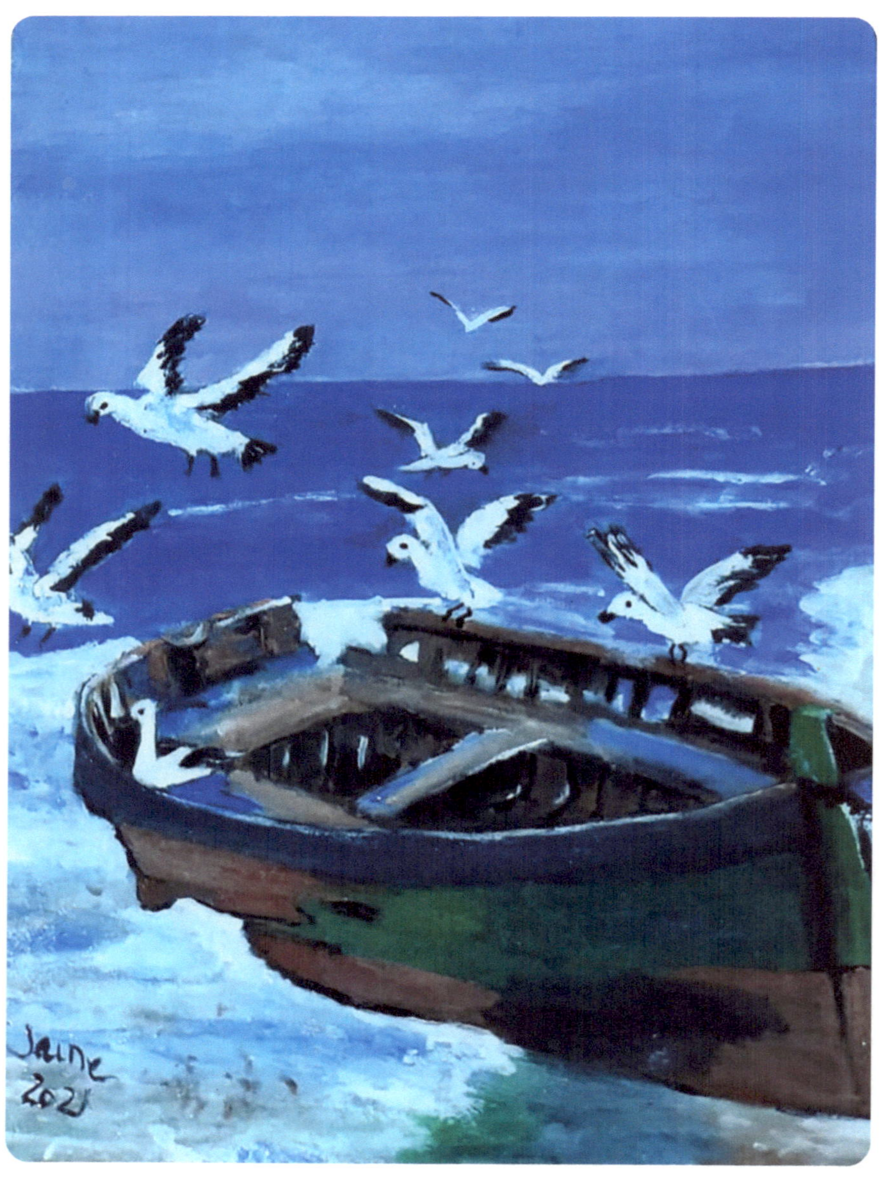

MOTHER.

Mother is there when you need a listening ear.

Just like the sea, we can hear.

Mother can get very angry, and one is scared of

what might happen?

Just like the roaring of the sea.

Mothers often sing sweet melodies around the house, and it

makes one relax.

Just like the tide rolling in,

Mothers sometimes disappear, not seen or heard.

Just like the calmness of the sea.

But most of all, my Mother is the best when she sees a red

sky at night and says,

Tomorrow will bring another bright and sunny day.

Just like a sunset, over the deep blue shining sea,

just like my Mother, who is bright and gay.

That always said she's on her way...

TO BE AWARE

The wind carries people's lies.
The wind absorbs the deceit and anger,
it can be felt in the air we breathe,
The mountains hold this pain within them.
The trees are the first to notice,
Their leaves fall as if they are weeping,
saddened by the lies of mankind.
What the wind blows onto its branches,
fills the earth with our mistakes, the leaves
fall prematurely,
The seeds that emerge are weaker,
and those that survive, not even they have any fragrance.
The roots are damaged even before they emerge,
Few survive due to poor quality,
The seedlings that do emerge are fragile, and very few survive.
Heal now.
Change your thoughts to vibrate with love,
so that the wind can carry them to the highest mountain,
let it blow over all to heal the earth,
So don't scream don't cry, the wind gathers everything and
carries it away. So think carefully about what you are going
to think,
so that the wind can carry your prayer well.

UNBORN

An innocent little child,

unborn,

never having tasted life.

Without the freedom to defend yourself.

In a world of rebellion.

Before your time,

You wanted to come,

But it couldn't be,

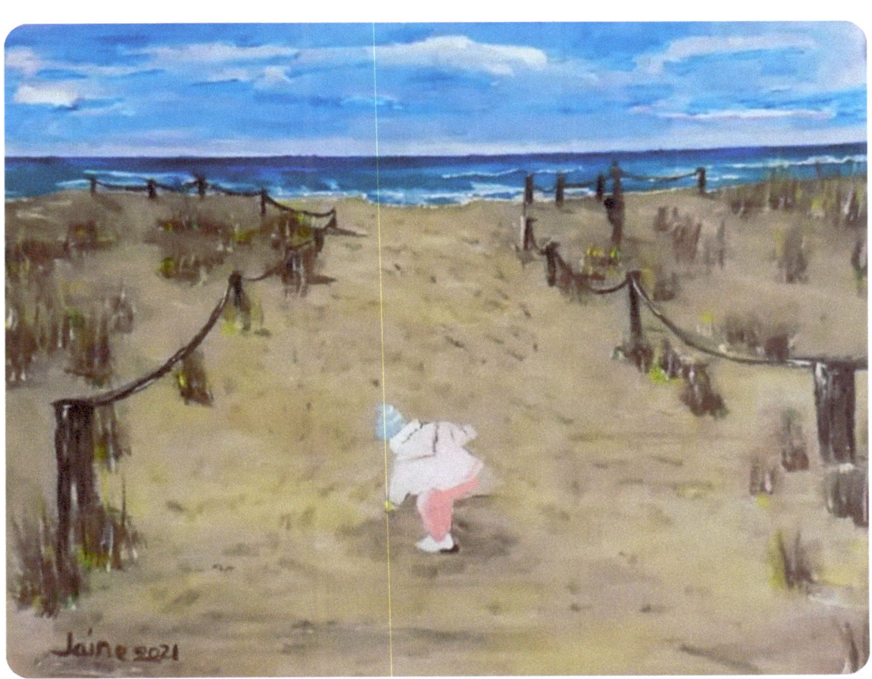

without seeing your face,
without smelling your fragrance of innocence,
without holding you in my arms.
But you remain inside me,
in every moment of my life,
a little child without a face,
without a body,
Yet for a brief moment, we shared my body,
my love, my dreams, i had a little angel inside me, and didn't,
know how to appreciate you o appreciate
the life that was growing within me,
I can't put a face to you,
But you are always in my thoughts,
day and night, and if i could give you a name,
It would be.
Julie Elaine...

BREATH

Life is but a breeze,

today i had you by my side,

This morning we sat together for breakfast.

Now night has arrived and you are no longer here.

Tear drops fall down my cheeks.

Suddenly you're gone.

I know you're waiting for me,

amongst the softest, sweetest cotton clouds.

In my life iv met many people and are no longer here,

They'll be waiting for me when it's my time.

Amongst the soft cotton clouds, you guide me,

and give me strength to keep going,

Your beautiful wings are your radiant light, stars twinkling

bright in the sky by night.i look up and there you are,

jumping and dancing with joy,

there you are in all your glory.

For all of us who know you, we wish you well. Life is just a

breeze away, and we'll be seeing you again.

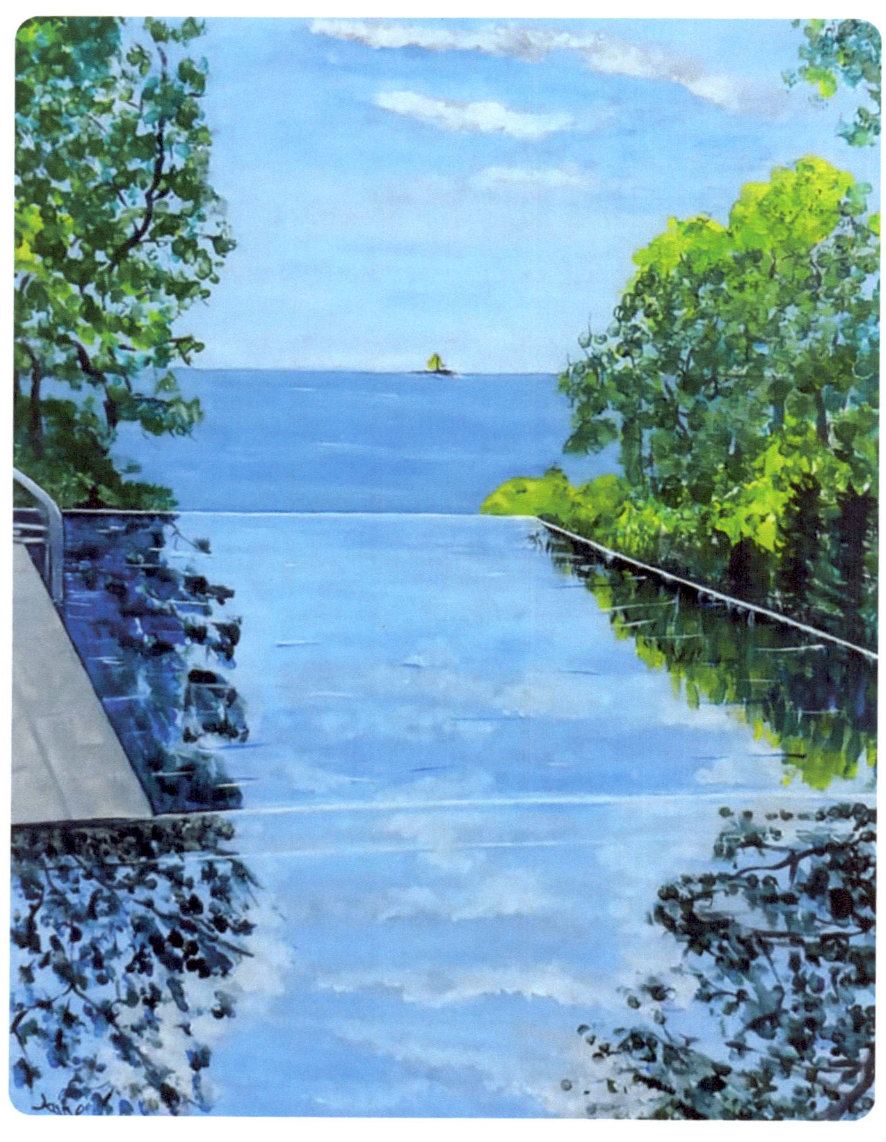

CYCLE OF LIFE

Time is running out.

We don't have time, not even to breathe.

Run, run, run, said the wind,

you don't have time to breathe.

The wind blows words to the mountains,

the mountains with a fright scream to the ocean

The ocean jumps in a shock and covers the earth.

That was once full of life.

Finally, normality is back.

Now there is time for all,

Time goes slowly. We have plenty of time in a day now.

Slowly, the wind blows harmoniously to the mountains with its

sweet melodies,

The mountains don't even move; They don't even groan.

Calmness is all around.

The sea feels the calmness of the mountains; it's like a clean

crystal sheet.

The Earth starts to grow once again.

Then the rain comes falling from the sky that has been

recollected from the sea so healthy.

All start to grow in harmony and love once again.

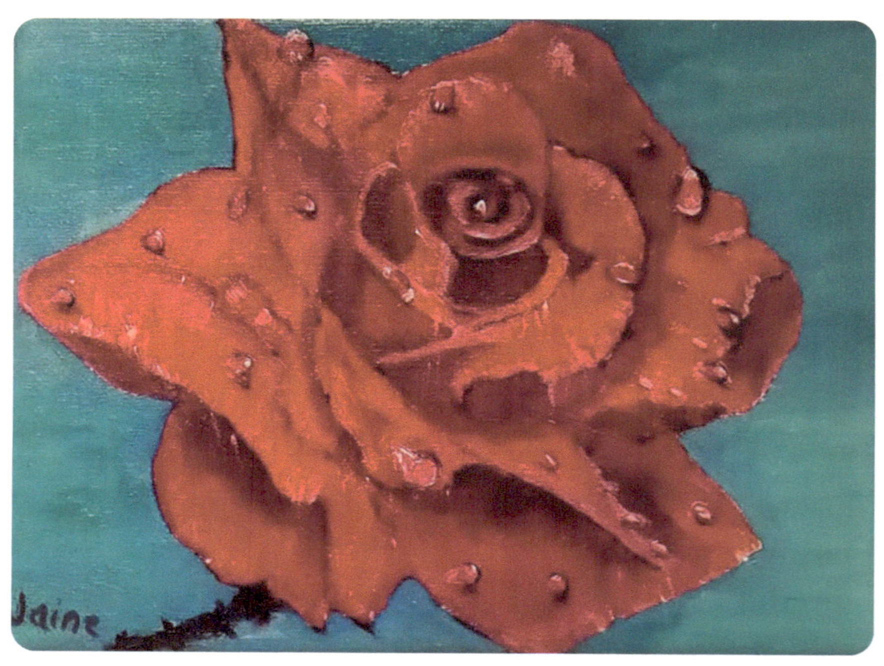

Jaine

I LOVE YOU FOR THIS.

Love doesn't come with instructions,

Love is a surprise every day.

The least expected moment,

someone will see your beauty,

and your craziness.

A friend loves you for your strength and energy to keep fighting.

Your mother loves you for the love that is part of her.

Your dog loves you unconditionally for being you.

Your cat feels your joy and sorrow.

And loves you so much, in your sadness,

it sits by your side and absorbs all your negative energy.

Giving you love again.

And finally, with so much love, a unique person enters your life,

who teaches you to love like you've never felt before.

How beautiful life is,

we are surrounded by love and affection,

and we can't see it.

It is right in front of us every day.

Good morning, world.

SWEET DAWN

Good morning, sweetness of dawn.

You that opens my heart, gentle sunshine,

You have gifted me with these vibrant colours,

They are like sparkles of light and rainbow colours, jumping and

sparkling on the surface of the sea.

Whispering hope of a new, beautiful day.

Here below this tree that is waking up from the long, cold night.

It filled with colours and sparkles of light,

from the day dawning and warming its trunk.

Below, I am here meditating, contemplating these wonders,

listening to the waves,

which do not stop whispering to the world.

!Good morning!

!Good morning!

Birds flying in the sky,

On the branches of the tree, the fledglings crying for food.

Here in the midst of all this beauty,

i sit quietly meditating,

The dew of the night is still touching my cheek.

It will be another bright and colourful day.

With my eyes, i see people walking in front of me,
I can see sparks of light jumping on their faces
forming rainbow jumping like sparks of gold round their bodies,
jumping from body to body, saying
"Here I am, the new day dawning."
that has arrived in your hands,
if only you could see,
it is all you need to be in the moment of this new day dawning.

VAIN WOMEN

I see you walking down the street,

with your back straight. Your head held high.

You are fragile.

It's scary to touch perfection.

That creation made it so untouchable for many.

Vain women,

You are aware that because of your beauty and height,

No one comes close to you.

They look at you when you let your hair down,

you move your head in style, letting it flow,

freely, flying in the wind, soft as silk side to side.

All staring at this freshness of being called young.

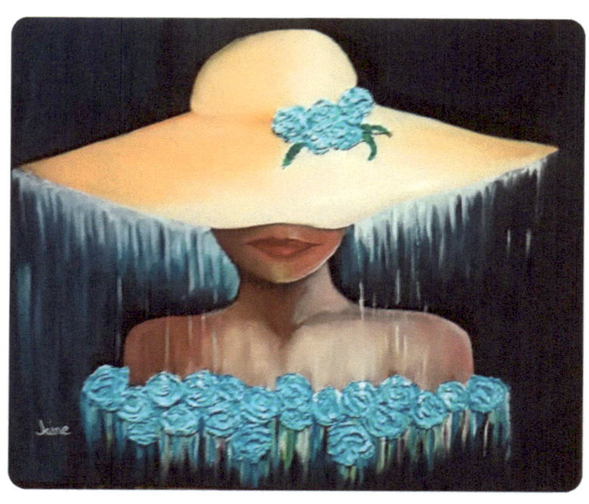

IF YOU

If you break my life, I'll rebuild it.

If you break my heart, I'll sew it back together again.

If you break my things. I'll buy them again.

Thats life.

I will get up again.

And start again.

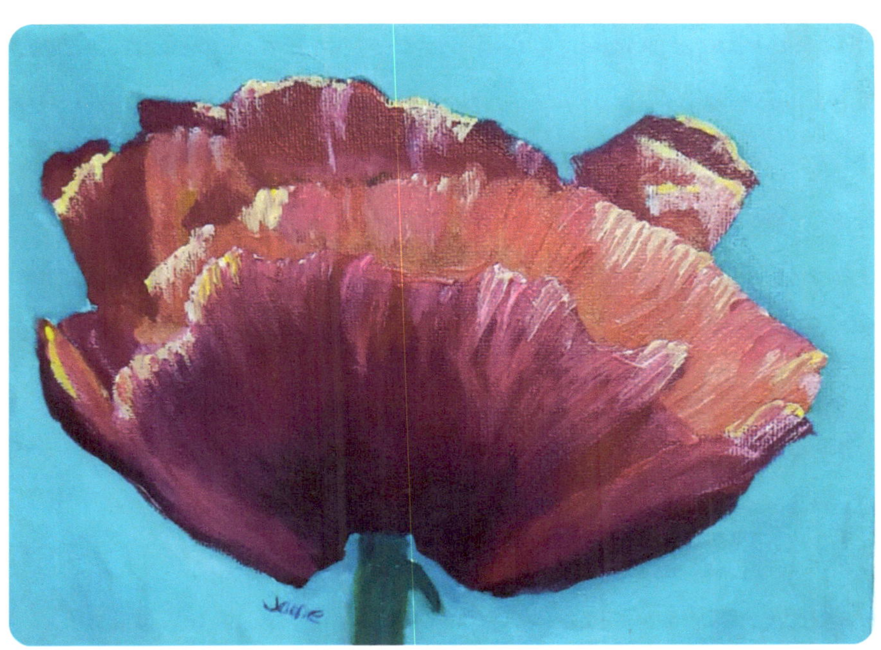

WHO WOULDN'T LOVE A SOUL LIKE YOURES?

Being a child all your life is a blessing, not a punishment.

And you know it,

women with the soul of a child, of innocent spirit,

It is a blessing to live happily with a soul like yours.

The world does not understand,

that is true.

So teach them.

Rebellious innocent girl, grown woman.

You have anger against the world that does not understand you,

with your childlike soul and such a tender heart,

responded with rage and wisdom that you know, for your age.

You have a lot of responsibility.

Do not get upset with the foolishness of your age,

for not understanding,

How simple life is,

You know how to forgive with love,

Your anger will burn with love,

Your disputes will burn with love,

Injustice will burn with love.

Who cannot love a soul like yours?
This is love.
Fighting in a world where children don't understand
You because you're different,
you're not stupid.
But you are smart because you know what you want in a world
where the children don't know what they want to do, and want
to be
"You do"
Your struggle is every day an infinite struggle, endless with ideas
to continue fighting and showing the world what you can do
with your innocent spirit.
That touches the hearts of many with your painting and
literature, you show us that nothing is impossible in your world
of innocence. Who would not love a soul like you?

A MOTHER AND HER SOLIDARITY

My daughter of my soul. My heart,

In my arms, you are warm.

I wish to truly love you.

I cannot tell you what i feel

i cannot hug you as i wish,

or love you as I want.

I cannot laugh with you.

I cannot.

Because of me, you are like this.

My heart is broken into pieces of loneliness,

no one understands,

a mother whose daughter was born this way.

Will never be a child of her age,

No one will understand.

I wish my world would go away.

My daughter whom i have in my arms,

whom i truly wish to love,

I wish i could close my eyes and have everything

disappear, and when i open them it had been just a dream,

And you are a child of your age.

IF I COULD

If i could die today.

I would,

I look out of my window and see nothing, feel nothing,

i see the emptiness in my life,

it can't be filled.

I know i can't recover,

so if i could die today, I would.

The emptiness eats me from the inside,

more each day.

The dryness of my mouth gives me away.

The tremors in my hands are noticeable.

If only for a moment. "in my thoughts"

If you died today, what would happen?

NO TIME

Your life, your time.
Your love for art.
Always time for te '
with notes of praise for her to understand
hearts beats time away,
hearts beat too fast at times and hide the pain,
a shiny note to raise the day,
a touch of darkness to say farewell.
To a day that bought a thousand
windy windy wirles.

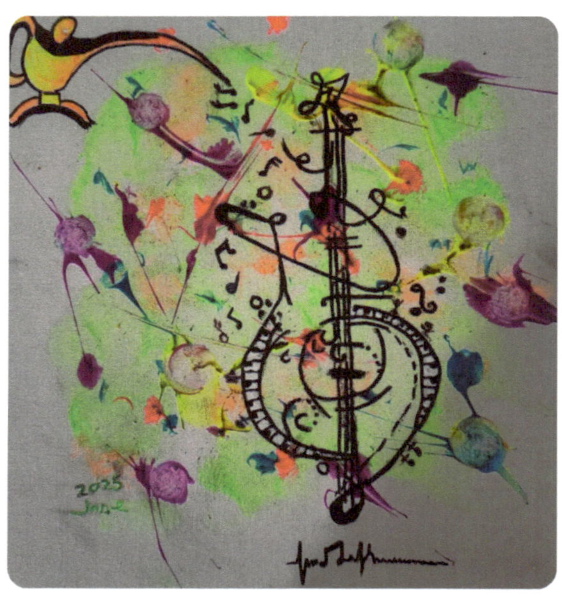

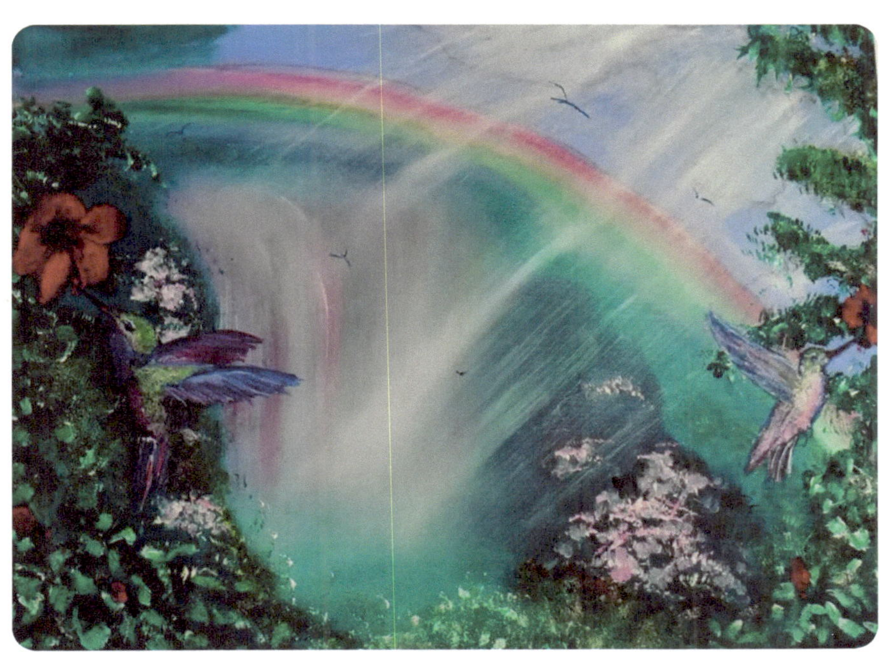

LITTLE GIRL

Little girl that i have in my arms at this moment in time.

You are looking into my eyes with tenderness, instant love.

Trusting me,

This moment is eternal.

There is no past and no future.

Just here and now.

Your thoughts and mine are united in this instance.

You're in my arms, my little girl.

For an instance in time, you are mine.

When you look at me with those little bright twinkling eyes and

trusting in me completely.

Your life is in my hands at this very instance;

There's nothing more. Than that. You, and me and the energy

of the world wrapped in our arms in a rainbow cloud.

To enjoy this moment when you are mine and I'm yours.

Neither the future nor present or past

can take away this moment you trusting me completely as if

you were mine and i was yours

WANDERER

This morning, going down to the sea.

I saw you hidden amongst the rocks,

lost in the current of life, wordlessly

For instance, our eyes met.

I saw your sadness and loneliness

in silence, from the waves of life,

frightened by the recklessness of not being able to do anything.

A woman of your stature, hidden in the rocks with your

rucksack, hidden from life.

This isn't the time to mourn, we all need to be together in this

time of destruction. Rage and disorder in the aimless world.

Aimless wanderer.

¿What happened to you, for you to be like this?

REFLEXIÓN

In my deepest thoughts,

I love this silence.

That I'm feeling inside me.

I love my thorns that are nailed,

with the love of disobedience,

I love this moment of reflection,

to heal my deepest emotions.

RICHEST MAN

He is sitting, watching the world go by.

I'm not a tramp.

I don't ask for anything,

I sit here in silence, reading.

People pass my path in front of me,

saying hello, good day,

how are you today sir, those who see me regularly.

But some stop,

and ask?

They are curious about my book.

A book that has no sense,

a book that is to catch the attention.

Of the people passing by.

So that the loneliness is less,

In this world, everyone is running alone,

waiting for an opportunity to speak

Here on the bridge that joins towns, I sit patiently waiting,

With my book. It's not just a book, it's a book of conversation.

To break the ice,

They stop and say ¿what are you reading, sir?

What a way to break the loneliness,

I don't ask for money, i only ask not to be

On my own,and to have a daily conversation with the world.

My home is a box and a cage with no one to talk to.

No windows to see out,

But on the bridge the world awaits me

whoever wants to talk.

Feel free to do so i'm here waiting.

The bridge is my home, the stairs are the hall that leads to where I sit, which is my dining room. Where I sit in this corner waiting for you to speak to me about my book, I have in my hands that I haven't finished reading yet.

I am the luckiest man in the world.

I'm neither rich or poor. I belong to the same universe as you.

And await your conversations every day with excitement.

THORN'S ON YOUR PATH

The thorns in your path.
Thorns that really hurt.
Thorns that are there,
to learn.
Like a lesson from your dad.

There are other thorns;
that are so deeply embedded.
They really hurt.
There is no way to get them out;
they just keep getting deeper and deeper.
Not even a scolding from father will help.

Beware then of thorns on your pathway,
They are growing in knowledge.
Waiting to learn.,

Well, now you know.
Will you let them grow,
or will you let them go
Leccion unsolved.

COLORFUL WORLD

Ho when i open my eyes for the long night's sleep,
i see the wonderful paintings of this world's art,
You have painted for our eyes to see
With your brushes, you use to paint our existences that
brightens our day.
wonderful colours made by creation every day.changing sceneries
beautiful for our eyes to enjoy.
I see your splendid glory, you have made for us
And here your creation in action to wake us up to joy
With your sweet melodies from outside my window to brighten
our days
And we know you are near us.
I enjoy seeing all these glorious things,
life's art abstracts are for all to see,
and all enjoy and to know we are not alone.

THANKYOU

Thank you for this day that was promised.

I have lived it to the full.

I felt my existence for a moment,

for this moment

can last an eternity.

If you let it.

Good night;

THE TREE AND LOVE

There are hundreds of branches on a tree

with hope for a new dream.

When love comes,

over time,

They break.

Without hope,

false promises,

lies and, deception

Then that fatal day arrives.

No more branches on the tree.

Not even with the tears of your existence can you

water it,

so that it grows again.

A sad existence,

that once offered so much beauty

It is left without scent or desire to grow.

The book closes.

IN MY DEEPEST SOUL

Here in the solidarity of my deepest soul.

I plant my thoughts that haunt me.

The past and the future.

The selfishness adds its touch.

To destroy my moment,

to sink into the depths of my pain.

The traumas strike again.

The memories keep rising,

to the surface,

only to attack me again.

What more can happen?

The selfish presents itself again.

To give the worst of me.

¿I'm not like that?

My present says,

I'm ok. What

happened here ?

LOVE

34

Whispering love in the wind.
Whispering love in the touch,
Whispering love every breath we take,
Love is the ray that comes out
of your navel to the universe.

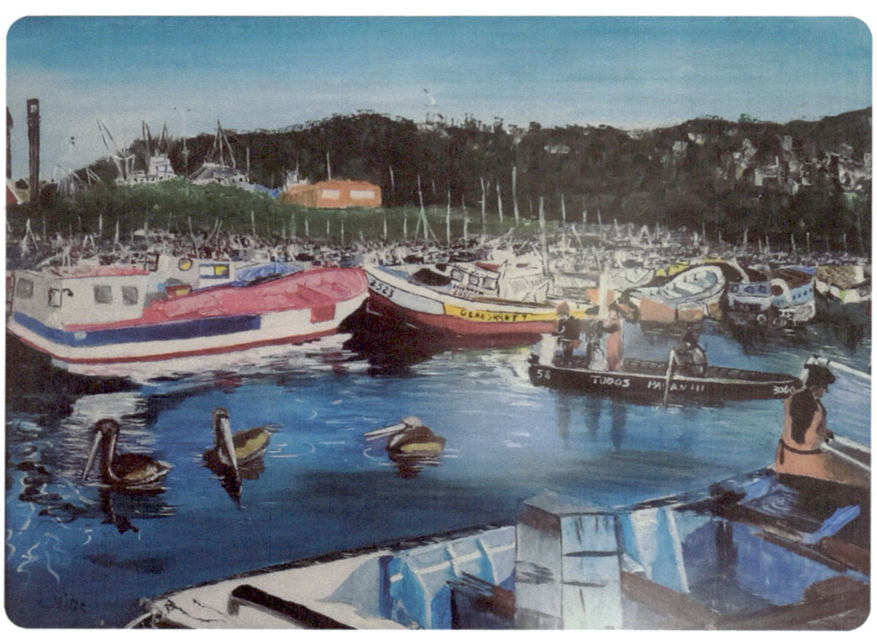

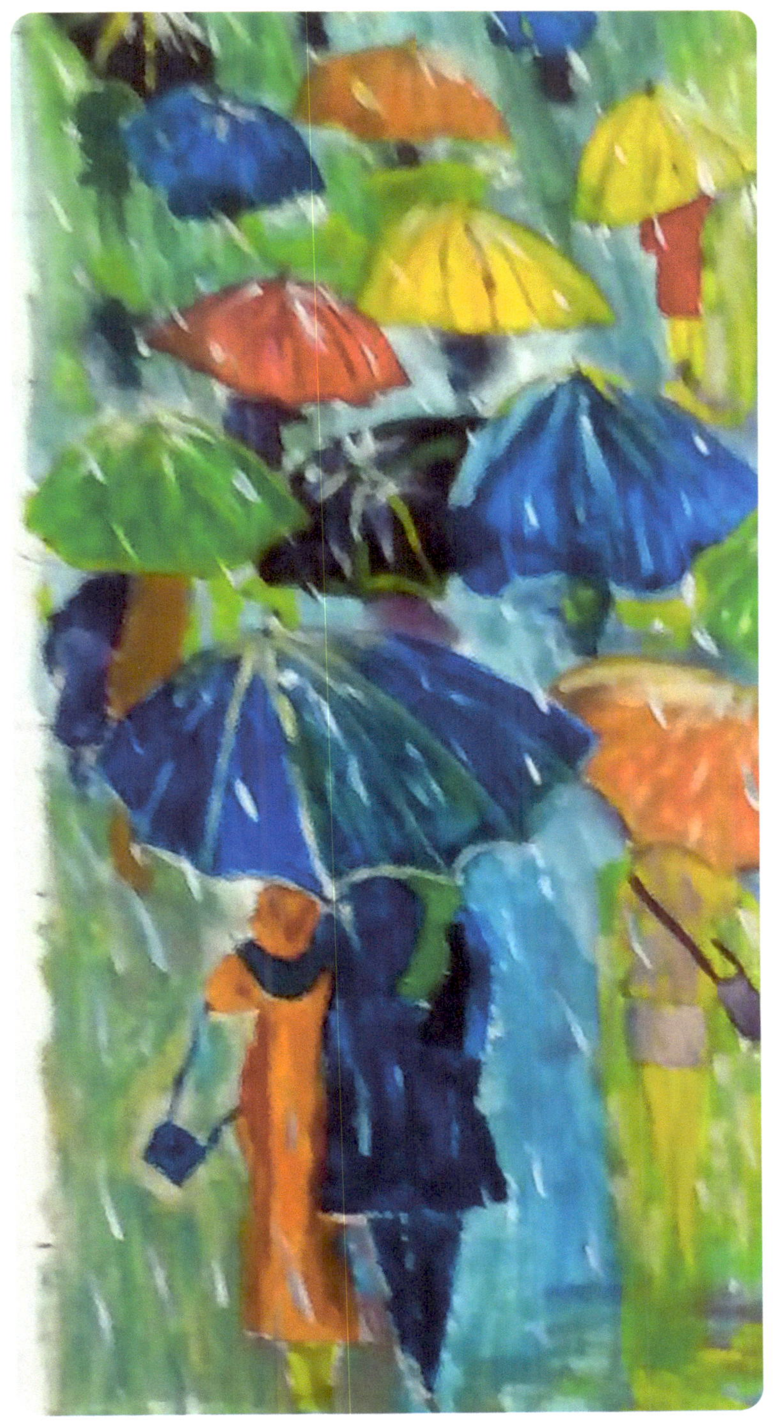

FOUR SEASONS IN TIME

Autumn.

Autumn winds that fly all away into the air we go, wirling, wirling away,

colours of autumn passing our way,

It's here to stay, just for a little while anyway.

To give us that freshness desperately needed after the long, hot summer days.

It's winter.

It has arrived with that coldness to freeze our cheeks

We know that for a while it's here to stay

With chimenias blasting we warm our bodies for a little while longer before we say spring is on its way.

It's spring

Here to our delight. We breathe the breeze of the air that was once cold and is now warm to our delight. All is blossoming for a while. We have this delight that spring is here to bring us joy for a little while longer, anyway.

The rain is falling hard now, just to let us know summer is on its way

and enjoy this little piece of rainbow happiness with the fresh raindrops falling, falling down on my cheeks just to let me know spring is nearly at an end and summer will soon be here and gone, It's here to enjoy for a while that heat of summer, the pleasure of the summer winds in the breeze of the sea make us know our year has come to rest and dazzle in the sun.

For a while anyway

It's all over, once again we begin. For a while, anyway. Autumn springs to be seen with those colours of autumn leaves falling to the ground.

Summer has gone once again.

WHAT INJUSTICE.

I see in your face that something is wrong.

"I don't know what it is."

I see into your lost gaze

that's something is wrong with you.

"I don't know what it is."

I see from the way you walk that you are not well.

And finally, you jump out at me,

stabbing me with a knife that penetrates my body.

"I still don't know what's wrong with you"

But the smell of your home.

The dirt in your home,

traps you

The i find the marijuana

That you had hidden from me.

Now i understand!

A man of your rank.

What has happened to you,

to fall into this well of no return.

The only one that cared about you?

you lost for a bit of weed you smoked.

To forget your madness.

A game you played with your wife,
That almost cost her life,
A man without direction,
with a heart of iron,
who doesn't feel?
Doesn't see the tears your wife cries.

CHILE PEPPER AND LOVE

You came into my life one day without expecting it.

With a chile pepper plant in your hand.

Love has finally arrived at this house.

The chile plant is the hope of a new love.

I have to water it every day,

must make sure it doesn't die,

if it dies, it's finished.

Year after year.

Look, the plant is in its splendour.

I'm so happy for this gift you gave me so many years ago.

The day arrived.

I woke up.

¿What happened? ¿What has happened?

Tears fill my eyes.

To day, everything will change.

I see the fruit falling endlessly.

I see the dry leaves,

¿What has happened?

Then came a call, and all was over, finished,

I don't cry because the chile pepper plant,

warned me.

That changes were coming.

SON

Ho my son you that are inside of me.
contemplando this moment,
our hearts beating in time.
our blood runs around
sharing this instant of interaction,
two souls as one.
You are there, hidden inside,
i can't see you.
In my head roamed around,
So many thoughts of you.
Are you ok my son that hides inside of me,
I can see you yes, you are part of me now.
My breath to live, you and me
inseparable from now on.
The day will come when you are ready,
the first face you see when you arrive,
will be mine.
I'm waiting for that moment to see you,
contemplating your movements inside of me
kicking me, i feel you turning inside, trying to run
but can't. Please my son, that is inside of me

don't rush. You have time.

I don't want you to come into this world before,

My hand touching my belly you inside of me

Don't be in a rush to come into the world

You are warm inside of me, I shelter you from the cold,

You have plenty to eat.

So don't rush to come out,

I'm ok

feeling you growing inside.

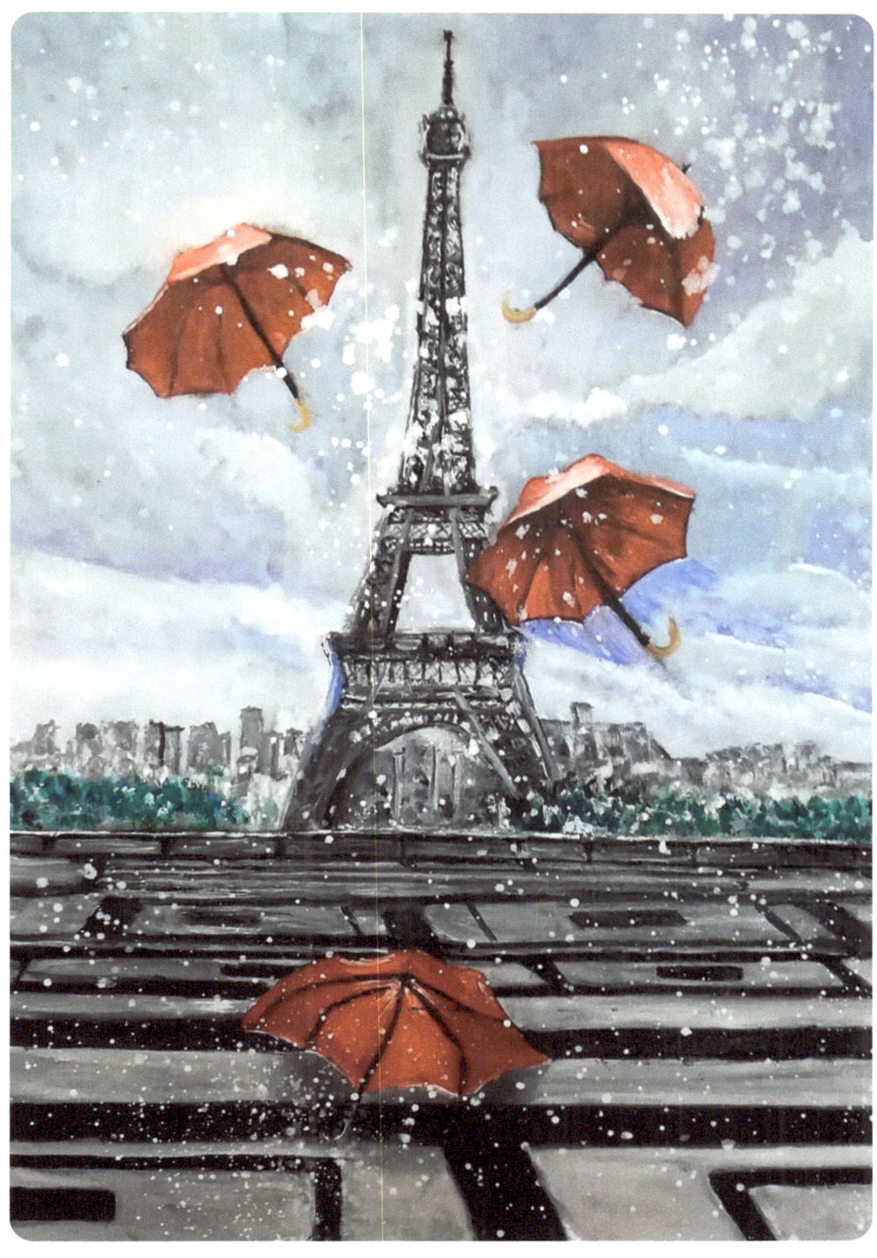

UNDERSTANDING

In a day, you flow with the wind,

soft to touch,

heart to heart,

You only feel the vibration of love,

the is no more

Forgive all,

small or large, thin or fat.

Forgive all.

There's no more to it,

Only misunderstanding.

When you learn to love

from the heart,

You see everything,

You feel everything,

In the end, we are strengthened by

understandable love.

FIN

45

The day i lost you is the day i woke up,

the day i saw everything but nothing,

I felt I had to just run, run and run.

So far from you.

Without understanding,

but free from this madness.

Now i only have tenderness

changing every day.

The past doesn't mix with the future to disrupt the essence of

perfection.

I have learnt,

I have grown as a person.

You will not trample on me again.

The love i have inside, not in the present time

does not know or understand the past cannot be mixed

It does not take the rage away,

But I will win the battles that are hidden inside.

DEFEND MOTHER NATURE

Today I want to defend Mother Nature.

Someone has to.

So here I am going to defend her.

¿Remember what happened with Noah and his ark?.

Well never again will she want that to happen.

So she made man wiser,

now we understand the technology

sufficiently better to warn us of another catastrophe that

happens in the world.

We need to change it normal, that the world also changes.

Mother Nature doesn't want us to suffer more than we should,

so she prepared wise men to control that and part. To warn us

of danger before it happens.

Like she did with Noah.

The problem here isn't ¿how can god do this to us?

So many deaths,

Mother Nature has made some men wiser,

to warn us before.

GRANDMOTHER.

Waiting for your arrival.

It's like an eternidad,

I came before time,

I couldn't wait any longer

Grandmother. Look where I am.

The sun that shines in the east,

with a gentle breeze and a sweet smell just like me

I come with health and strength and hair that I didn't expect.

In your presence, we communicate without words so as not to

be afraid

I know you will understand.

I am the ray that shines for you.

Soon I will speak with words of wisdom. That's before my time,

But with prudence and with you by my side, I will be fine.

But for now, I will enjoy my childhood and my parents, who

love me so much.

Here in my cradle, I am safe and at peace with angels by my side.

I see bright lights everywhere, i see their splendour

in their faces, and they are looking at me with tenderness and

love, i am surrounded by love in this cradle in which I am safe.

Grandmother, i am waiting for your arrival and to see your

bright lights by my side.

FROZEN TEARS.

48

Frozen tears frozen in time.

Of pain and unjust

tears frozen in time until the day we can go out.

Frozen tears falling from my cheeks.

To be thawed with rage and anger.

That fades in an instant, and the

pain is seen no more through

the freedom we were given

to be able to go out again.

A TORNADO.

I enter your lives like a tornado,

and yet you still accepted me.

Like a whirlwind that scares you,

and yet you still accepted me.

Without knowledge or understanding

and you still didn't abandon me

I am like nothing you have seen before.

You had to be patient because

What was knocking at your door,

was a bombshell of surprises

and yet you still accepted me.

and what a surprise,

you accepted this tornado aimlessly.

NIGHT'S SLEEP

In the silence of the night
they come in your dreams.
Steal your thoughts.
And put theres.
In the silence of the night.
When all are asleep.
Be aware.

LOOK AT YOUR WORLD

The sea never stops,
it's not always the same,
It's changing,
so learn to flow like the sea.
Without thinking, without stopping.
This is ok.
Look at the birds singing in the trees,
they don't have to learn anything.
They know, and they're happy.
There's nothing else they know, and that's that.
We make our own laws.
And that makes it difficult.
¿is it so difficult to understand?
Do your feet know what to do?
While walking in the river.
They do it, and that's that.
Is the feeling of knowing good?
Does the air know it has to blow?
It just does it and that's that.
Does the heart know how to think?
The heart only feels,
so when we think is when we lose the essence to act.
What a long road we are on to walk in the right understanding.

ASK

Look at the rain as it falls from the trees

Nature is wise.

And it knows their needs.

So look closely at your lives,

You are no different.

It gives you something too.

Don't ask for more than you need,

ask for just that,

and leave something for others.

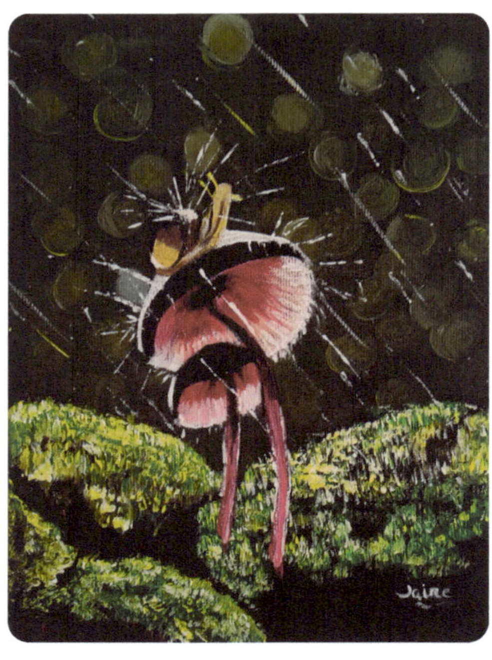

¿WHY DO YOU ATTACK ME?

I am like a tree planted in the earthly world.

¿because ?

I am earthly,

I am part of your world,

You take care of me, you give me water,

I see everything, I feel everything.

If you cut a branch,

I don't get angry,

if it's to burn and warm you from the cold night air,

I forgive you.

Another one will grow

in its place but stronger.

You come to sit under my branches,

hiding from the bad weather,

You meditate with me, while I protect you

You come to hide in my branches

When a person is sick, he comes to rest his feet on my trunk,

a channel of energy

a healing light.

I am planted firmly in the earth and say nothing.
I hear all your prayers, your doubts, and your dreams.
I don't answer, i feel your pain,
your sadness, your happiness too.
When you were children, you would climb me, you'd
listen to the air whistling in my branches. And laughter was
all around.
I am made of wood. You can burn me, and i'll still forgive you.
You can cut me down. I won't cry with this wood, you'll
turn me into your home to protect you and hide you.
The trees are planted to give protection and let you breathe.
¿Why do you chop me down?
I won't get angry with you.
As I live with you in your home.

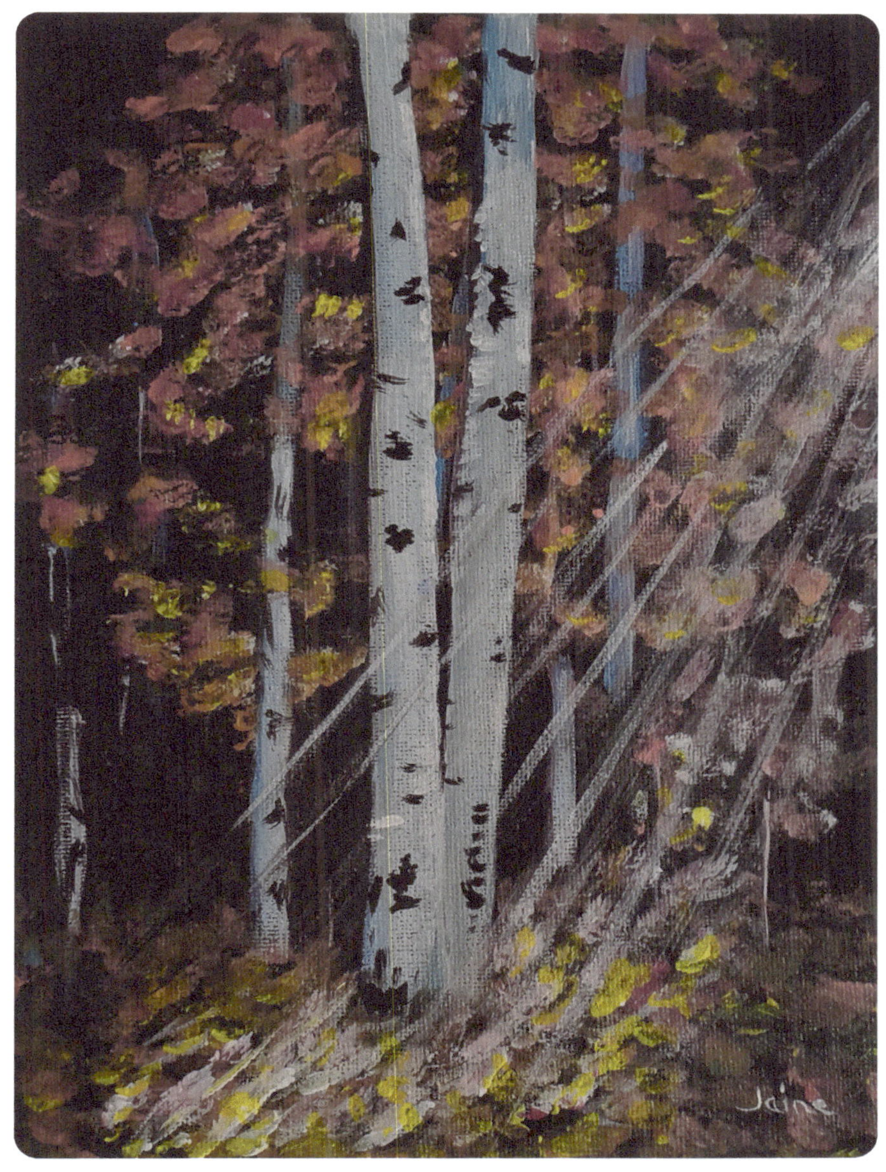

MOTHER NATURE SPEAKS.

Every so often, Mother Nature goes crazy,
like it wants to destroy everything it has built in a century,
It seems it doesn't want us to move forward.

Well, "look", just like families who have their loved ones by their side.
When everything starts going well for you, someone comes along to
destroy your world and your happiness.

Just like the dark side of Mother Nature,
We all have this inside us and can't change it.

Just listen and see what they want you to see.

Mother Nature says,
You can't beat me because you are all the same as me.

This, i fear, is anger and unjust. The wise men knew.
They prepare us well.
Waiting for Mother Nature to put order back in life.

You blame one another,
You don't see the destruction you're causing,
You don't see the suffering doctors,
who has to choose between who lives or who dies

You know what, they don't say in the media
the doctors die of desperation
So as not to see the outcome of what they can't change

Now you can see Mother Nature so angry with you, all look.
What Mother Nature has to put up with you all,
Now you are feeling pain like Mother Nature is feeling.
destroying her home, the earth.

Now you are all alone.

You cannot hug each other,
or kiss each other,
or meet with your families.

Mother Nature's defence.

You have torn my children from the earth, the trees the
animals, i also cry
and you didn't give me time to say goodbye.
So don't attack me because you attacked me first.
There will be a time of balance,
Think before you punish me. Think before killing one of my creation
I created it all for you to enjoy
Don't destroy nature then. The caves are your refuge, do not
kill my children of the earth.

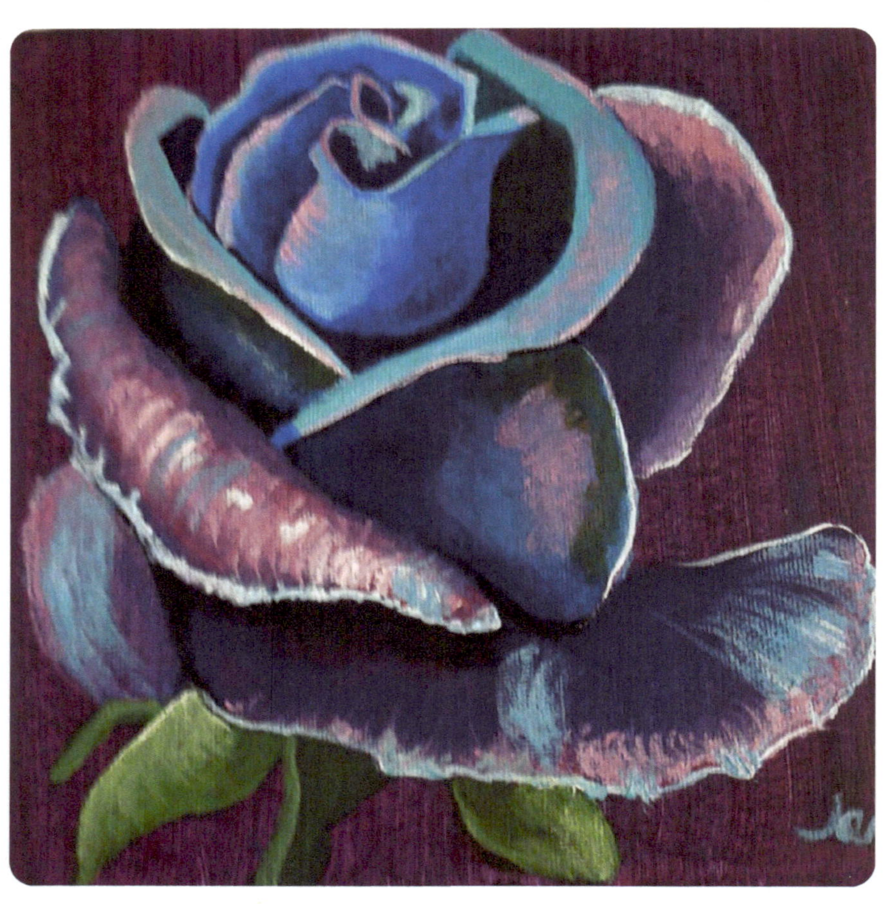

BEAUTIFUL ROSE

Life is beautiful,

just like a rose.

We are born beautiful.

As a rose in all its splendor,

to give us joy with its beauty.

And its smells of puberty, is unique just.

like a newborn baby.

Like the rose opens her petals to give the freshness of life,

We open our lives to grow and walk with the

innocent beauty of life's way.

Then one day, we look in the mirror to see

we have grown old, and we cease to exist.

Just like a rose when its petals start to fall,

and she knows it is time to rest her beauty.

That falls on the floor.

BELIEVE IT OR NOT

I lay my head down at the end of the day.

I have done enough.

More i can't do,

if you don't listen to what i say.

I said it. I told you.

Believe it or not.

It's up to you.

But at the end of time,

don't say you weren't told.

You know, but you didn't want to listen.

MY THOUGHTS.

In the darkness of the day i ponder,
here and there,
In the far distance, i can hear a whisper in the wind
calling me but i can't see
The fog is so dense, only a faint voice.
This way, must I go? Is going that way correct?
Then a voice starts again, this way two roads one destine
Think before you move?

We must move in wisdom then.
Wisdom takes us higher, and we glide along.
In the air, wisdom lingers around with the energy of the
universe, which holds us tight as not to fall into any trap life
puts in front of us.
So wisdom and knowledge is ours for the taking to glide through
life's expectations.

OUR PLANET.

Our planet is a special home.

I look up in amazement at the sky at night.

I see the moon and stars, and sometimes,

Get a glimpse of a planet.

And I wonder what wonders await me tomorrow.

From Mother Nature.

Every day she prepares a beautiful painting.

For us to enjoy.

When we go to sleep in the evening,

Mother Nature is thinking. What beauty shall I bring tomorrow?

For their eyes to see, and the smell to smell,

and the ears to hear the sweet melodies of hearing the grass whistling in the wind and the trees. Rippling like waves on an ocean shore,

backwards and forth. The hummingbirds get the sweet pollen from the flowers.

The bees make the sweet honey for us to enjoy.

Can you hear, can you see, can you feel nature in her splendour,

for us all to enjoy. Colourful pictures every day.

Even the rain has its beauty and leaves a rainbow as a surprise,

Mother Nature always surprises us, but also plays tricks on us too.

So we are never bored. Of a new day dawning.

There are always surprises painted for us.

So we just need to look closer and feel and see.

The brushes that paint our day.

And wipe it clean in the evening

to say there will never be another so splendid as today.

As tomorrow will be painted in a new and beautiful way.

INDEX